Aspects of P.E.

Health-related Fitness

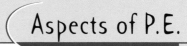
and Kirk Bizley

Heinemann
LIBRARY

www.heinemann.co.uk/library

Visit our website to find out more information about Heinemann Library books.

To order:
- ☎ Phone ++44 (0) 1865 888112
- 🗎 Send a fax to ++44 (0) 1865 314091
- 🖥 Visit the Heinemann Bookshop at www.heinemann.co.uk/library to browse our catalogue and order online.

First published in Great Britain by Heinemann Library, Halley Court, Jordan Hill, Oxford OX2 8EJ, part of Harcourt Education. Heinemann is a registered trademark of Harcourt Education Ltd.

© Harcourt Education Ltd 1999, 2007
The moral right of the proprietor has been asserted.
Revised edition first published in paperback 2008

Editorial: Andrew Farrow
Design: Joanna Hinton-Malivoire
Picture research: Hannah Taylor
Production: Alison Parsons

Originated by DOT Gradations Ltd
Printed and bound in China by CTPS

ISBN 978 0 431 07875 5 (hardback)
11 10 09 08 07
10 9 8 7 6 5 4 3 2 1

ISBN 978 0 431 07882 3 (paperback)
11 10 09 08 08
10 9 8 7 6 5 4 3 2 1

British Library Cataloguing in Publication Data
Mullan, Nuala and Bizley, Kirk
Health related fitness. - 2nd ed. - (Aspects of P.E.)
612'.044
A full catalogue record for this book is available from the British Library.

From Kirk: to Tasha, Jason, Sarah and Dean

Acknowledgements
The publishers would like to thank the following for permission to reproduce photographs:
Agence Vandystadt/Jean-Marc Loubart p**25**; Allsport p**32**; Allsport/Adrian Murrell p**37**; Allsport/Didier Givois p**36**; Allsport/Gary Prior p**41** Allsport/Gray Mortimore p**33**; Corbis/Leo Mason p**39**; Corbis/zefa/Pete Saloutos p**6**; Empics/Barrington Coombes p**38**; Empics/Tony Marshall p**19**; Eye Ubiquitous/Bennet Dean p**20**; Eye Ubiquitous/Paul Thompson p**23**; Format/Melanie Friend p**9**; Format/Sheila Gray p**10**; Fotopic p**14**; Getty Images/Stu Forster p**40**; Getty Images/The Image Bank p**4**; Getty Images/Taxi p**17**; Getty Images/Phil Walter p**29**; Getty Images/Stone p**16**; Harcourt Education Ltd/Gareth Boden pp **18**, **45**; Robert Harding Picture Library/L Wilson p**7**; Sally & Richard Greenhill pp**5**, **8**, **11**; Sporting Pictures (UK) Ltd p **35**.

Artwork p**31** by Big Top.

Cover photograph of a young woman on a climbing wall reproduced with the permission of Getty Images/MedioImages.

Every effort has been made to contact copyright holders of any material reproduced in this book. Any omissions will be rectified in subsequent printings if notice is given to the publisher.

The publisher would like to thank Kirk Bizley, Keith George, Lee Herrington, Paul Holmes, Trevor Lea and Doug Neate for their comments in the preparation of the first edition, and to the Manchester Metropolitan University for their support given to the author.

Contents

Any words appearing in the text in bold, **like this**, are explained in the Glossary.

What is health?

The World Health Organization (WHO) has defined health as 'a state of complete physical, mental and social well-being, and not merely the absence of disease or infirmity'.

Many people tend to associate poor health with being sick or ill, and good health with being well. However, health also involves mental health and social well-being. Some people may not have any particular illness but their quality of life may not be very good.

- *Physical health* involves being free from illness and being fit enough to be able to do the things you want to do.

- *Mental health* involves feeling good about yourself, having a positive attitude to life and being able to cope with everyday stresses and strains.

- *Social well-being* involves being able to interact with people around you in a positive way.

Your health is affected by many factors. Some of them are individual things, such as fitness levels, but others relate to your surroundings.

Exercise and health

Exercise is good for your health because of the physical changes that it brings about in your body, but being active can also be beneficial for your mental health and social well-being. Exercise can make you feel good and can help reduce stress levels. It can also be a great social activity. For many people, this kind of physical activity is a way of going out and meeting other people, and it enhances the quality of their lives.

Sometimes exercise can help prevent a disease or reduce the effect it has on a person's health. **Coronary heart disease**, **obesity**, **osteoporosis** and back problems are all common health concerns. They can all be helped by regular exercise.

Coronary heart disease

The heart is a working muscle and, just like any other muscle, it needs a good supply of oxygen. The heart is surrounded by a network of blood vessels, called arteries, that carry oxygenated blood to all the parts of the heart muscle. Arteries also carry oxygenated blood around the rest of the body. In some people, fat gathers on the walls of the arteries and this can restrict blood flow. The medical name for this build-up of fat is **atherosclerosis**. People who smoke, eat a lot of fatty foods or are inactive are at greater risk from

Many people go to a gym to keep fit. Treadmills are a popular alternative to running on the streets and roads at night and in bad weather.

Heart disease

Heart disease is the main cause of death in the UK. About one in five men and one in six women die from coronary heart disease each year: that's over 100,000 deaths a year. Although the rates are falling, they are falling faster in many other countries. In more developed countries, only Ireland and Finland have mortality rates that are higher.

Obesity can cause many health problems

atherosclerosis. When this happens in the arteries of the heart, it is called coronary artery disease or heart disease.

Obesity

This is a medical term applied when people are carrying excess levels of body fat. Obesity can cause problems because the heart has to work harder to get oxygen around the body and to move the body's weight around. The extra weight that is being carried also puts an added strain on the joints.

Obese people have a higher chance of getting cancer, heart disease, diabetes and other health problems. Exercise and diet are the main ways to control or reduce body fat.

Anorexia

Anorexia is an eating disorder characterised by an obsessive desire to lose weight by refusing to eat, or eating only very small quantities. Anorexia can cause many physical problems because the body is not receiving the correct balance of nutrients required to keep it in good working order.

Osteoporosis

This condition, which affects the bones and causes them to break more easily, is often called brittle bone disease. It is very common in older women who have gone through the **menopause**, which means that they have stopped having periods. After this their bodies produce less of a hormone that helps protect bones, so breakages are more likely.

Exercise can help maintain bone strength and limit the effects of osteoporosis. Many women have been prescribed **hormone replacement therapy (HRT)** by their doctors to prevent osteoporosis. However, the benefits of HRT are being questioned as it has been related to side effects, such as an increased risk of breast cancer.

Back pain

Every year many working days are lost because people are off work with back problems. Pain in the lower back is a common complaint. It is often due to poor **posture** and weak stomach and back muscles. Exercise, such as pilates, can help improve muscle tone, which improves posture, and can also help to increase the strength of the stomach and back muscles.

2 Health-related fitness

Fitness has been defined by the World Health Organization (WHO) as 'the ability to perform muscular work satisfactorily'. The level and type of fitness will depend on the type of physical work to be performed:

- Performance-related fitness means being fit enough to do an activity as well as possible. The activity might be a sport or form of exercise or part of a job.

- Health-related fitness means being fit enough to do everyday activities and to live a full and healthy life.

Most aspects of general fitness are part of both performance-related and health-related fitness to some degree or other.

Components of fitness

Health-related components of fitness include:

- Body composition – the percentage of body fat and **lean body mass** (anything that is not fat) that make up the body. High or extremely low body fat levels can affect health.

- Aerobic endurance – the ability to keep exercising while using oxygen to supply energy. A reasonable level of aerobic endurance is important for health in order to allow you to do everyday activities and to limit the effects of disease.

- Balance – the ability to keep control of the body's movement.

Swimming is an excellent form of exercise. It can be enjoyed by most people, at their local pool or while on holiday.

- **Strength** – this can be divided into three types:

  - **maximum strength**: the maximum force produced in one effort. Strength is needed for many everyday activities;

  - **muscular endurance**: the ability to perform repeated muscle contractions without tiring. Activities such as walking require a level of muscular endurance;

  - **power**: a combination of strength and speed. It is the ability to exert high levels of force over a short period of time. This is less important from a health point of view but there are activities such as climbing stairs that require a basic level of power.

- **Co-ordination** – the ability to put together a series of movements in an organized manner.

- **Flexibility** – the range of movement at a joint or series of joints. A lack of flexibility can prevent people from doing certain activities.

- **Speed** – the ability to move the body, or parts of it, quickly. Like power, speed is less important from a health point of view, but a basic level is still required for good health.

- **Agility** – the ability to perform a movement of the body, or part of it, rapidly. This requires elements of speed and flexibility. It also plays a part in preventing a fall.

There are a wide range of activities that can help improve all of these aspects, and there are several tests for measuring fitness, for example the 'bleep test' (see the panel on the right).

Hill-walking is a good way of keeping fit.

However, health-related fitness is not just about fitness tests. You need to be aware of all the factors that affect your health, so that you can take steps to reduce the chances of getting illnesses and injuries. These factors are explained in the next chapter.

Bleep test

One of the most common tests of fitness is the 'bleep test'. Its proper name is the progressive shuttle run. It tests the endurance of the **cardiovascular** system. The person being tested carries out various sets of shuttle runs against pre-recorded timed bleeps over a 20-metre course. The higher the level of 'bleeps' a person can get to, the greater their level of fitness.

3) Factors affecting health

Health and health-related fitness are closely linked and they affect each other. The body's health and fitness are affected by:

- biological factors
- physical environment
- social factors
- personality
- lifestyle.

Age is a biological factor that affects health.

Biological factors

Although you cannot change biological factors such as age, gender and race, it is important to be aware of how they can affect your health and fitness.

Age

As you get older, changes that occur in your body affect your health and fitness. **Aerobic endurance**, strength and **flexibility** all decrease with age. The decrease in aerobic endurance is mainly due to inactivity and weight gain. It can occur from the age of 20. This will limit the amount of physical activity that you can manage and can make everyday tasks more difficult. Housework, gardening and generally moving around can become much harder. Older people may need help with these tasks; some may need other people to care for them. This can be very frustrating for people who have been used to doing things for themselves. Many of these changes can be avoided or slowed down by keeping physically active and following a healthy diet.

Gender

Gender affects people because some health problems are more common in men than in women, and vice versa. Up until the age of 75, **coronary heart disease** is far more common in men than in women. After this age, men and women are more equally at risk.

In contrast, osteoporosis is a disease of the bones that affects women more than men.

Ethnic differences

Some health problems are more common in certain ethnic groups. For example, there is a high rate of coronary heart disease in many groups of people living in countries other than their homelands. The level of coronary heart disease is higher in South Asians living in the UK. For Afro-Caribbeans living in the UK, the incidence of coronary heart disease is lower, but there are higher rates of high blood pressure and stroke. The reasons for these differences are not yet clear, but they could be connected with diet, lifestyle or biological factors.

Some diseases can be inherited. This means that they are passed on from parents to children. However, most diseases tend to be a combination of inherited (genetic) factors and environmental factors.

Physical environment

The physical things that surround us, such as air, water, roads and noise, can affect health. Some health problems related to aspects of the physical environment, such as **water** quality, have improved over the years. Other health problems have become worse because of the deterioration in the environment.

Water

Poor water supplies can encourage the development of some diseases. Household water supplies are treated and monitored to make sure they are clean enough for consumption. This means that water-borne diseases are now fairly rare. However, in less developed countries, unclean water can be a major source of disease.

Roads

In the last 25 years, road traffic has increased by over 80 per cent, leading to increased congestion, especially in cities. Although the number of deaths and serious injuries has fallen in this time, road safety is one of the government's major health concerns.

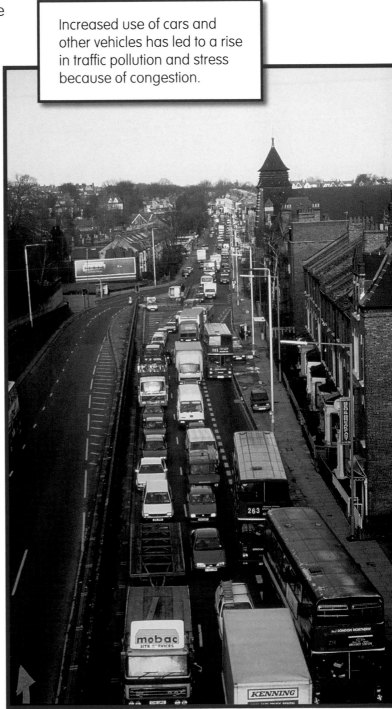

Increased use of cars and other vehicles has led to a rise in traffic pollution and stress because of congestion.

Noise

Continuous exposure to high levels of noise can damage hearing. Employers have a duty in law to protect their workers' health, and so many companies insist that their workers wear ear protectors in noisy areas.

Noisy neighbours can also affect a person's health. Although the noise may not be enough to damage hearing, it can prevent people from getting enough sleep and cause a level of stress. This may affect a person's physical and mental health.

Air quality

Many factors can affect air quality and cause health problems. Car exhaust fumes and factory emissions pollute the air with chemicals. This is a particular problem for people living in large cities where the pollution is usually greater. Changes in the weather can make matters worse. When there is a fog, the chemicals emitted from cars and factories mix with the fog to produce **smog**. As you approach a big city, you may sometimes see smog hovering above it. Because smog reduces air quality, it can cause health problems.

Air quality is also affected by natural things. Pollen produced by certain plants can cause particular problems for people with asthma or hay fever, making breathing difficult. These problems affect so many people that the weather reports on television, radio, the internet or in the newspapers now give an indication of whether the pollen count is going to be high or low.

During physical activity you breathe in more air than when you are at rest, which means that the air quality can have a greater effect on your body. Many people who cycle to work in cities now wear face masks to filter the air that they breathe.

Pollution

The amount of pollution produced by industry is monitored. Companies must ensure that the waste products their factories produce cause minimum damage to the environment.

Occasionally, something goes wrong with these procedures and a lot of damage is caused to the environment. The release of harmful waste products into the air can mean people have to stay indoors until the air has cleared. Spillage of waste can also cause massive problems. The waste can get into water supplies or into rivers, lakes and the sea. It is often the local wildlife that suffers the most harm.

Factory emissions can pollute the air with chemicals.

Social factors

Social factors include a person's family situation or who they live with. Having a happy home life is an important part of feeling good and being healthy. Other social factors, such as employment, income, housing and education, relate to your economic situation.

Having a job and enough money are important for physical and mental health. Being unemployed can cause people to feel badly about themselves and this can result in depression. Poverty can mean a lack of good food and heating, and this can add to stress. People with lower incomes may not be able to afford to take part in physical activities that cost money. Poor housing and damp, and cramped conditions will also affect health.

Personality

Your personality affects how outgoing you are and your motivation to be healthy and enjoy life. It also relates to your psychological well-being. If you have a positive attitude to life, you are more likely to look after your health. Previous experiences will affect your personality. If someone has had a lot of unhappy experiences in life, they are less likely to feel good about themselves and will probably be more anxious about things than other people. These experiences can relate to areas such as health and exercise. Unhappy experiences are likely to have a negative effect on your health.

Lifestyle

This is the way a person chooses to live and how they behave. Many of the current health problems throughout the world are a result of people's lifestyle, and could be reduced by changes in behaviour. Health is affected by lifestyle factors such as:

- physical activity
- hygiene
- smoking
- alcohol
- drugs
- diet.

Maintaining good health can enable you to enjoy your life better.

4 Physical activity

Physical activity and exercise are recommended as part of a healthy lifestyle, so it is important to understand what these terms mean. Physical activity is the most general term. It includes any activity that involves movement and requires more energy than is needed at rest. Physical activities include:

- housework, gardening and cleaning cars and bikes;
- moving around – walking and climbing stairs;
- exercise – sport, dance and many outdoor activities.

Exercise is a type of physical activity. It is often taken in leisure time, and usually for enjoyment or to keep fit. Exercise may be taken in the form of:

- walking – hill-walking and walking a dog;
- jogging or running;
- dancing – ballet, ballroom, latin, line and folk dancing are all popular forms of exercise;
- aerobics – various forms of aerobics, including step and aqua aerobics, have been popular for many years;
- working out in a fitness gym or weights room;
- swimming, gymnastics, cycling and all forms of sport.

There are many other types of exercise. Sport is a controlled form of exercise, with rules, regulations and competitive structures.

Levels of physical activity

In 1990 the Allied Dunbar National Fitness Survey was carried out in England. In this survey, thousands of adults between the ages of 16 and 74, from different parts of the country, were interviewed and fitness-tested. The results of the survey showed that only the

Gardening is a physical activity that can improve fitness

following percentages were active enough to benefit their health:

- 24–29 per cent of men in different age groups;
- 8 per cent of 16–34-year-old women, 14 per cent of 35–54-year-old women and 26 per cent of 55–74-year-old women.

This meant that, on average, about seven people out of ten were not sufficiently active to benefit their health. The survey also found that most people thought they were more active and fitter than they actually were. This meant that a lot of work needed to be done to encourage people to be more active and improve their health-related fitness.

Although there have been many activity surveys since the 1990 one, they have not been as statistically reliable and carried out on such a large scale. However, if the 1990 survey was done again, many health professionals would expect similar results.

Health education

There are many health promotion organizations in the UK, including charities such as the British Heart Foundation. NICE (the National Institute for Health & Clinical Excellence) is the independent body responsible for providing national guidelines on the promotion of good health and on the prevention and treatment of ill health.

Until the 1980s, a lot of the work that many of the health agencies and charities did was not related to physical activity. However, everyone now accepts the evidence that links physical inactivity to various health problems, so in recent years these organizations have emphasized the role of physical activity and fitness in promoting health.

Physical activity at work

Manual workers (such as builders and road workers), professional sportspeople and teachers of aerobics do a lot of physical work and, therefore, need a lot of energy. There are other jobs that involve a lot of walking or moving around. Postal workers, traffic wardens, waiters and waitresses, and those looking after young children also use a lot of energy, although probably not as much as people in the first group.

Many other jobs involve relatively little physical activity or exercise. These are called sedentary jobs. Office workers, truck drivers and check-out assistants in supermarkets are examples of people with sedentary jobs.

Increases in technology mean that people do not have to do as much work as they used to. Washing machines, car washes, lifts, escalators and cars all cut down the amount of physical work in people's everyday lives. This means they need to increase activity levels in other ways.

Prescribing exercise

Physical activity is now recognized to be so important that GP's are 'prescribing' exercise to patients as a form of treatment. This can include taking part in specific sessions in leisure centres and health clubs. There have also been recent moves to enrol patients in slimming organizations to help them lose, monitor and maintain their weight at acceptable levels.

Benefits of exercise

The benefits of exercise or physical activity can be:

- sociological

- psychological

- physiological.

Sociological benefits

These are the social benefits gained from physical activity. Families and friends can enjoy spending time together doing some sort of physical activity. People also meet new friends through taking up a new activity or exercise. Being active will also help you to remain mobile and independent as you become older. This can have a major effect on your social situation and well-being.

Psychological benefits

These are the mental benefits, such as improved mood. During exercise your brain releases certain hormones that actually make you feel better and improve your mood. Exercise can also help improve your **self esteem**, which is the way you feel about yourself. Many people exercise to keep a trim figure and a positive body image.

Cycling is a good way of improving aerobic endurance.

Physiological benefits

These are the physical benefits of exercise and physical activity. There are many ways in which increased physical activity and improved fitness can result in health benefits. The degree of health benefits will depend on:

- how much activity you do
- your level of fitness
- the type of activity you do
- your age.

Here are some of the general benefits and how they relate to health.

Body composition

High levels of fat are linked to health problems such as **coronary heart disease**, cancer and joint problems. Aerobic exercise is a good way to help control body weight. During a session of light exercise, lasting around 20 minutes or longer, it is mainly fat that is used to supply the energy. This can help you to lose excess body fat or maintain a healthy body weight.

Aerobic endurance

Doing regular aerobic activities such as walking, cycling, swimming and dancing regularly improves your **aerobic endurance**. Changes occur within your body that mean that you can do aerobic activities more easily. These changes include:

- lower resting heart rate
- lower heart rate for a given work load
- faster recovery rate after exercise
- greater ability to use fat for energy
- increased ability to take in and use oxygen that allows the muscles to work harder.

Through regular exercise, your heart is able to pump out more blood per beat and your muscles are able to take more oxygen from the blood than before. This means that your heart does not have to beat as often to get enough oxygen to your muscles. As a result, your resting heart rate and your heart rate for a given amount of work are lower. Your recovery from exercise is faster and your body is able to take in and use more oxygen. The overall effect is that your aerobic endurance improves. This means that:

- you can cope with more strenuous activities than you could before;
- you can do a lot of activities with greater ease than you could before;
- you recover more quickly after physical activity or exercise.

After you reach the age of 20, aerobic endurance can start to decline. However, by keeping active, this decrease can be slowed or prevented.

Aerobic exercise increases the efficiency of your **cardiovascular** system, so it can help prevent diseases of the heart and circulation. An active person is less likely to get coronary heart disease because their heart works more efficiently. However, even active people can have heart attacks, but they are more likely to survive them than people who have been inactive.

For people with **hypertension** (high blood pressure), exercise can help reduce blood pressure. However, for people with very high blood pressure, exercise can be dangerous because they may not be able to cope with the extra strain exercise puts on the heart. People with hypertension need to consult a doctor before doing strenuous exercise.

Strength

Strength decreases with age, which means that many older people do not have enough strength to do everything they want to do. Activities such as lifting and carrying become more difficult or impossible, due to decreased **maximum strength**. Lower levels of **muscle endurance** also affect the ability to do repetitive movements and mean that **fatigue** sets in earlier. Levels of **power** are also affected due to a decrease in strength and speed. Together these changes can have a dramatic impact on a person's lifestyle.

By keeping active, you can slow down or even prevent the decrease in your strength, muscular endurance and power. Correct **posture** is an important aspect of health. Your **muscle tone** is developed when your muscles are stretched, and this helps to maintain posture. Physical activity can help improve muscle tone and hence posture. Physical activity will also help improve the control of movement.

Balance and co-ordination

Balance and **co-ordination** are important as they allow you to make a series of movements. Walking, climbing stairs and most other activities require balance and co-ordination.

Flexibility

You tend to lose **flexibility** as you get older. This means that you find things like reaching up to get something from a shelf, or reaching down to put shoes on, more difficult. This can have a major effect on the quality of your life. You may become dependent on others, and this limits your freedom and affects your health. Regular exercise will help prevent the decrease in flexibility with age and allow you to remain independent for longer in later life.

Dancing classes or social dancing, whether modern or traditional, are an excellent form of exercise and an enjoyable way to meet other people.

Speed and agility

Speed and agility are not usually considered essential for health but being able to react and move quickly can be very important. Speed of movement can help prevent accidents. If you come off the kerb while walking along a road, it is partly your speed of movement and agility that allow you to recover quickly and not fall. One of the reasons elderly people have more falls is because their speed and agility have decreased with age.

Bone strength

Exercise can help maintain your bone strength. This is particularly important for older people as their bones tend to weaken with age. This problem, called **osteoporosis**, is very common in older women.

How much exercise do you need?

There are two main exercise recommendations that have been made by health bodies such as NICE and the American College of Sports Medicine:

• Original recommendation – vigorous exercise at least three times a week for 20 minutes each time.

This is the amount of exercise needed for maximum improvements in aerobic endurance and to reduce the risk of death. However, many people feel that this is too much for them to do. The second recommendation is based on the fact that even moderate levels of physical activity can improve health.

• New recommendation – at least 30 minutes of moderate exercise at least five days a week.

This may seem to involve more exercise than the first recommendation but there are two key differences that make it easier for people to achieve:

• The physical activity is moderate, so walking, cycling and gardening count.

• The 30 minutes can be split up into smaller amounts such as two fifteen-minute sessions. You could take fifteen minutes to walk to work and walk back again after work every day and you would have reached the recommended level.

Whichever recommendation you follow depends on your current level of fitness and how fit you want to be.

Moderate exercise, such as walking the dog, can improve health.

6) Hygiene

Personal hygiene plays an important part in keeping yourself healthy, and it can also affect those around you. Hygiene includes:

- personal cleanliness
- dental care
- washing clothes regularly
- handling food properly
- preventing infection and disease.

Personal cleanliness

It is important to keep yourself clean in order to reduce your chances of becoming ill. You can come into contact with dirt and germs in many ways and these can lead to health problems. Following these guidelines will help ensure you keep clean and healthy:

- Wash your hands several times a day, for example after going to the toilet, to avoid the spread of germs.
- Have a shower or bath regularly, especially after doing any exercise that has made you sweat. This will clean the dirt or sweat from your body and help you feel refreshed.
- Wash your hair regularly to ensure it stays clean and healthy.
- Clean and cut your finger and toe nails regularly to prevent dirt building up under them. This can also help prevent the development of ingrown toe nails, which can be very painful.

If you do not wash regularly your body will start to smell unpleasant. This is called body odour (BO). Deodorants and antiperspirants can help to hide BO, but the only way to avoid it is to wash or have a bath or shower regularly.

It is important to have a shower after exercise that has made you sweat heavily.

Dental care

It is important to look after your teeth because once you lose them they cannot be replaced. As well as brushing your teeth at least twice a day, especially after meals, you can also take care of them by avoiding sugary foods that can cause tooth decay.

You should visit the dentist for regular check-ups, normally every six months, so that problems can be identified and treated quickly. You often can't tell you have a dental problem until it gets painful and then it may be too late for the dentist to save the tooth.

Washing clothes

You should change and wash your clothes regularly, especially your underwear, because they gather dirt and sweat from your body and the surroundings. This is especially important after exercise. Because you sweat more during physical exercise, many people wear a special set of clothes, such as sports kit. Even if your clothes are not covered in mud or do not look dirty, they should be washed because they will be sweaty and might spread infection into cuts and grazes.

Food hygiene

Although the general standard of hygiene has improved in society, food poisoning is a significant problem. This is because a lot of food is processed and can be kept longer, but if food is not stored or handled properly, bacteria can spread and cause illness. Washing your hands before handling food, cleaning kitchen surfaces and utensils properly, following storage directions and use-by dates, and cooking foods properly, can all help prevent food poisoning.

Preventing infection and disease

Following the above recommendations will help prevent a lot of health problems. The proper care and treatment of cuts and wounds will help prevent infection. It is also important that if you have an infectious disease you are careful not to pass it on to anyone else. Your doctor will tell you what to do if you have an infectious disease, and it is important for other people's health that you follow this advice. Some diseases, such as malaria, food poisoning and cholera, must be reported to environmental health officers so that they can take action to identify the source and prevent them spreading.

As part of the Government's efforts to prevent disease, babies, children and young people are given special vaccinations or inoculations. These are usually given by injection but some are taken orally. Some, such as tetanus, need to be renewed after a period of time. Vaccination builds up your immunity to a

disease, so although you may still get the disease, you are unlikely to get it so badly. Vaccinations are given for a variety of diseases such as German measles (rubella), polio, tetanus and whooping cough.

Before you go abroad you might be given some medicine or injections to prevent you from getting diseases that are common in the country you are visiting. This might be in countries where the level of hygiene and control of disease is not as good as in more developed countries.

These players will need to wash themselves and their kit thoroughly after the game.

Smoking and alcohol

Smoking and drinking alcohol are two forms of behaviour that can damage health. Drinking alcohol in moderation is not necessarily bad for you, but drinking excessive amounts is bad for health. Smoking, on the other hand, is always bad for your health.

Smoking

Although it has been proven that cigarette smoking is very harmful to health it is still a common habit among many adults and young people. For example, the percentage of men and women in England who smoke has gradually decreased over the last 25 years from around four or five people out of every ten to around two or three people out of every ten.

However, the percentage of young people (11–15-year-olds) who smoke has stayed at about one in every ten for many years. Smoking cigarettes:

• reduces resistance of the lungs to disease and often causes cancer;

Health warnings

Governments in most countries require that each packet of cigarettes sold must contain large health warnings such as 'Smoking kills'. This is to ensure that smokers are aware of the health risks, to themselves and others, that are associated with smoking.

• results in coughing (smoker's cough), sore throat, shortness of breath and chest problems;

• irritates the passageways of the lungs and gradually destroys their lining;

• increases airway resistance making breathing harder;

• can be harmful to the baby of a pregnant woman;

• can decrease fertility.

Moderate alcohol consumption is not necessarily bad for health, but smoking is.

Smoking also increases the oxygen cost of exercise because the body needs extra energy for breathing. A substance called carbon monoxide in cigarettes combines with the red blood cells in the blood and this affects the amount of oxygen that can be carried around the body.

There is a lot of evidence to suggest that non-smokers' health can be affected when they inhale other people's smoke. This is called **passive smoking**. Because of this, smoking in enclosed public places, such as restaurants and work places, was banned in Scotland in 2006 and the rest of the UK in 2007. These bans follow similar decisions made in parts of Europe and the United States.

The ban has been welcomed by health organizations and most non-smokers. It is hoped the ban will improve the nation's health significantly and reduce the costs to the National Health Service of treating smoking-related disease.

Alcohol

Drinking alcohol is a social habit enjoyed by many adults. Going to a pub or restaurant with family or friends can be a pleasant way to spend some leisure time. Drinking moderate amounts of alcohol does not necessarily do any harm. However, drinking a lot of alcohol can damage the body and affect its health. Alcohol is broken down by the body in the liver and can damage the liver cells. The effects of alcohol can be short-term or long-term.

Short-term effects

- Alcohol impairs the nervous system. This slows reaction time and affects **co-ordination**, **balance**, speech and hearing.
- It acts as a depressant.
- The liver and kidneys have to work harder.
- It may cause stomach upset and vomiting.
- Blood vessels in the skin dilate (widen) and heat is lost, which may cause chilling.

Long-term effects

- Damage is caused to the liver and the brain cells
- High blood pressure and strokes
- Stomach problems
- Heart failure
- Infertility
- Alcohol addiction may develop.

Alcohol affects balance, co-ordination and reaction time, so people should not drink alcohol before physical activity. If they do, they are more likely to have an accident or injury. Many people go for a drink after physical activity to relax and talk to each other. However, drinking alcohol might cause dehydration. This means that the body does not have enough water to function properly. It is a good idea to drink plenty of fluids after exercise but alcohol is not suitable.

Don't give alcohol

Many people think that giving alcohol to a person who is cold will help warm them. In fact, the opposite is true. Alcohol causes the blood vessels in the skin to dilate (widen). This means that more heat is lost, which makes the person even colder.

8 Drugs

Drugs are chemical substances that affect the way the body works. Medicines are drugs that can prevent and cure disease.

Many medicines, such as headache tablets, can be used easily and safely if guidelines are followed. These medicines are available from chemists and supermarkets. Other medicines need to be controlled more because they could do serious harm if they are not used properly. These medicines are only available on prescription from a doctor and they can only be supplied through a chemist or pharmacy. Many people rely on medicines to keep them alive and healthy. Unfortunately some medicines that are prescribed for a good reason can become addictive. Sleeping tablets may be prescribed for someone who is having difficulty sleeping, perhaps due to stress or illness. However, if the pills are taken for too long the person may become addicted to them.

Side effects

Used correctly, drugs can help treat particular health problems. However, nearly all drugs have some other effects, called **side effects**, which can be undesirable. Some people suffer worse side effects from certain drugs than others.

Drug abuse

Using drugs when there is no health reason for doing so, or taking more of a drug than is needed, is called **drug abuse**. It can be very harmful to health.

Drug abuse has become a major problem in society. Many people misuse drugs to escape from reality and to get a 'high' feeling. However, the side effects of most drugs are serious. This is why the use of drugs is controlled by law. Some drugs, such as alcohol and nicotine (the drug in tobacco), are subject to certain restrictions for young people. Alcohol cannot be sold to people under 18 years of age, tobacco to those under 16. Others drugs can only be used for medical purposes and some are illegal to use or supply. Anyone found breaking these laws can be prosecuted.

Sport and physical activities are not free from the drug abuse problem. Some players misuse drugs to try to improve their performance. These are called **performance-enhancing drugs**. In recent years many athletes have been caught taking drugs of this type. This gives them an unfair advantage over other competitors. They are banned by the World Anti-Doping Agency (WADA). Some of the most commonly abused drugs in sport and exercise are:

- stimulants
- beta-2 agonists
- anabolic agents
- narcotic analgesics
- beta blockers
- diuretics and other **masking agents**
- hormones and related substances

Stimulants

These drugs increase alertness, wakefulness and the ability to concentrate. They may increase a person's ability to exercise strenuously or decrease their sensitivity to **fatigue**. This is dangerous because the symptoms of fatigue are the body's way of saying that it cannot continue with the demands being put on it. If a person does not respond to these symptoms, the body

Some busy office workers abuse amphetamines to help keep them alert.

will be pushed beyond its limits. Then injury, dehydration or even death could occur.

A side effect of stimulants can be to make the user more aggressive and hostile. They can also affect **co-ordination** and decision-making ability, which can lead to accidents.

Amphetamines (pep pills) are stimulants that are used widely. They have been used medically to reduce appetite. Caffeine, which is found in tea, coffee and cola drinks, is another stimulant. Many people drink these every day. This may be to enjoy them as pleasant drinks, or it may be to help them keep awake and working longer. Amphetamines have been used by airline pilots to help them stay awake and by people studying for exams or under pressure at work so that they can go without sleep. This practice is not good for health as it deprives the body of the sleep it needs.

Many stimulants are banned for sports performers, and there is a limit to how much caffeine they are allowed to have in their body before a competition. Many stimulant substances are also found in medicines, such as treatments for hay fever, asthma and

colds, so athletes need to be careful about using them. Cocaine is a stimulant drug and it is illegal to take it or to possess it.

Beta-2 agonists

There is an unusual group of stimulant drugs known as beta-2 agonists that is classed as being both stimulants and anabolic agents. They have anabolic effects and can have similar side effects to stimulants.

Stimulant side effects

Common side effects include:

- increased hostility

- loss of judgement

- high blood pressure and headaches

- strokes and increased and irregular heartbeats

- anxiety and tremors

- insensitivity to injuries

- addiction

Anabolic agents

These drugs are the ones commonly abused by sportspeople. Anabolic agents can be synthetic (artificially made) compounds, similar to the male hormone testosterone, or extracted from animals. They have two types of effect on the human body:

- androgenic effects – promoting the development of male characteristics

- anabolic effects – helping the healing and build-up of muscle tissue

There are many forms of anabolic agents, often known as steroids. They can be taken in tablet form or injected into the muscle. Steroids are not just abused for sporting reasons. Many young men take steroids to try to make themselves look more muscular.

Some athletes have misused steroids because they believe they increase their muscle strength, allow them to train harder and increase their competitiveness. There is a lack of strong evidence that they do actually increase strength except in young males (before puberty) and in females. Anabolic agents are banned from most sports. They are often difficult to detect because they are taken during training periods and if stopped before a competition can be harder to detect. Anabolic agents, such as steroids, have some very serious side effects:

- General – they cause damage to the heart that can lead to increased blood pressure, heart attacks and strokes. Liver damage can lead to jaundice, liver failure and tumours. They encourage water retention (bloatedness) and they increase the risk of some cancers. They also bring mood changes such as increased aggression, irritability, moodiness and depression.

- Men – effects include reduced sperm production and infertility, along with decreased sex drive.

- Women – effects include growth of facial hair, irreversible voice changes (deepening), infertility and acne.

- Children – stunted growth.

Narcotic analgesics

These are painkilling drugs that can hide the effects of injury or illness. Narcotics put people to sleep and analgesics kill pain. Because of this, athletes who use them can push themselves beyond their normal pain threshold. This can be dangerous. They can be used medically to treat pain but are banned for most sporting events.

Codeine, morphine and heroin are types of narcotic analgesics. Athletes are banned from using them. Codeine is a common ingredient of cough mixtures and cold remedies, so athletes need to be careful which ones they use. Morphine and heroin are extremely addictive. Morphine can be used for medical purposes but the misuse or possession of heroin is illegal.

Side effects of narcotic analgesics include:

- headaches

- dizziness and confusion

- exhaustion or over-training

- addiction.

Beta blockers

Beta blockers used to be prescribed commonly for people with heart problems because they reduce heart rate and blood pressure. Because they lower heart rate they have a calming effect. This can benefit performers who have to keep calm and hold a steady position, such as in snooker, archery and shooting. In other sports this effect would be of little benefit and could be dangerous. These drugs are banned from sports where they could affect performance, and should only be taken if prescribed by a doctor.

Diuretics

Medically, diuretics are used to remove excess fluid from the body and to help treat high blood pressure. They are used by sportspeople to reduce weight rapidly, especially those competing in weight categories such as in boxing and the martial arts. In many sports, urine samples may be taken before a competition to check for the presence of drugs. Some athletes take diuretics to increase the production of urine and dilute it, making it harder to detect other drugs. For this reason, the use of diuretics and other masking agents is banned.

Hormones

Certain hormones and related substances can be misused to increase the body's levels of the hormones and steroids that can have an effect on performance.

Doping control

More about banned drugs can be found on the website of the World Anti-Doping Agency (WADA). The use of drugs to improve performance is cheating, and so is banned. There are procedures to try to catch those who abuse drugs. The process is called doping control.

Blood doping

Blood doping increases the number of red blood cells in the blood so that more oxygen can be carried. This helps increase aerobic fitness. Blood is removed from the athlete and stored for a time. During this time the athlete's body makes more red blood cells to replace those it has lost. The stored blood is then transfused back into the athlete to increase the number of red blood cells.

Ben Johnson (left) was banned for drug abuse after winning the 100 metres in the 1988 Olympics in Seoul, South Korea.

9 Diet

A good diet is important for health for everyone, not just sports performers. Any healthy diet should include a variety of different foods that allow your body to function at its best. These foods can be put into five main groups, based on what the foods contain. The main food groups are shown in the diagram on page 31.

There are three important concepts for healthy eating:

- Variety – different foods provide different nutrients. Eating a sufficient variety of food will help ensure you have a healthy diet.

- Balance – eating the right amounts of different foods is vital for a balanced diet.

- Moderation – eating too much or too little of any one food group or nutrient might be harmful.

You eat food in order to supply your body with the nutrients it needs. The six essential nutrients are:

- **carbohydrates**
- **fats**
- **proteins**
- **vitamins**
- **minerals**
- **water**.

The food that you eat is broken down into smaller pieces by the digestive system. These smaller compounds are then absorbed into the bloodstream and taken to the cells that need them. The food can be stored, used to provide energy or excreted from the body as waste products.

Carbohydrates

Carbohydrates are important for maintaining your body's energy stores. The two main types are:

- **simple carbohydrates** (sugars)
- **complex carbohydrates** (starches)

These are digested and used for energy. Dietary **fibre** is also a form of carbohydrate but it is indigestible.

Simple carbohydrates (sugars)

Simple carbohydrates are made up of a few sugar units. The most common are glucose, fructose, lactose, sucrose and maltose. Jam, marmalade, honey, sugar, sweets and biscuits are all rich sources of simple carbohydrates. They are less nutritious than complex carbohydrates because they contain smaller amounts of other nutrients.

Complex carbohydrates (starches)

These are made up of many sugar units. Foods such as bread, rice, pasta and some vegetables, such as potatoes, are valuable sources of complex carbohydrates. They are considered a good source of carbohydrate because they also contain vitamins, minerals and fibre.

Fibre

Fibre is not absorbed by your body but it is essential to ensure the digestive system works properly. It is the non-digestible carbohydrate that forms the skeleton of plant cells. Good fibre sources include wholegrain bread, whole wheat pasta, brown rice, cereals, **pulses** and fruit and vegetables.

Fats

Fat is an important nutrient but it is generally believed that people eat too much of the wrong sort of fat in their diet. This can lead to **obesity** and related health problems such as **coronary heart disease** and cancer.

Fats are major sources of energy. They also help our bodies to absorb important vitamins. Fats are stored in the body and provide insulation and protection as well as energy.

The main types of fat are:

* **saturated fats** – mostly found in meat and dairy products, as well as cakes and biscuits. Too much saturated fat can increase the chance of developing high **cholesterol** and heart disease.

* **trans fats** – these are sometimes made in the food manufacturing process and found in biscuits, cake and fast food, as well as some margarines. They can have similar effects to saturated fats.

* **unsaturated fats** – these can be a healthy choice. Oily fish, nuts and seeds, as well as sunflower, rapeseed and olive oil and spreads, are all high in unsaturated fats.

Proteins

Proteins are needed by your body for growth and repair of tissues such as muscle, hair and skin. They are also used to make enzymes (see page 28) and hormones.

Proteins are made up of simple units called **amino acids**. Your body does not normally use protein to provide energy for exercise, but in extreme conditions such as starvation it might. Also during very long periods of low-intensity exercise, protein may be used when carbohydrate supplies are running very low.

There are 21 amino acids, most of which can be made by your body (**non-essential amino acids**). There are at least eight **essential amino acids** that your body cannot make so they must be obtained from the diet. Animal sources of protein, such as meat, fish and dairy products, contain all the essential amino acids but tend to be high in fat. Vegetable sources such as beans, cereals and pulses are high in carbohydrate and fibre but contain lower amounts of some amino acids. You require a mixture of these foods for a balanced diet.

Vitamins

These chemical compounds are needed only in very small amounts by the body. Vitamins cannot be made by your body so they must be eaten. There are two classes of vitamins.

* Fat-soluble vitamins – vitamins A, D, E and K. These are stored in relatively large quantities in your body. Too much of these vitamins can be harmful.

* Water-soluble vitamins – mainly vitamins B6, B12 and C. These are mostly involved in the body's energy processes. They are not stored well in the body so need to be consumed regularly.

Carbohydrate levels

Carbohydrate is the most important fuel for exercise but the body can only store a limited amount of it in muscles. Therefore, it is important that people involved in physical activity eat enough carbohydrate every day to keep their stores at the right level.

Vitamins are needed for a variety of purposes and can be found in different types of food:

- Vitamin A is important for sight and for the maintenance of skin and connective tissues such as tendons and ligaments. Good sources of vitamin A include green leafy vegetables, eggs, carrots, dairy products and liver.

- Vitamin B comes in a variety of types. It plays a key role in energy processes so it is an important vitamin for anyone who exercises. Vitamin B can be obtained from meat, liver, fish, dairy produce, grains and green vegetables.

- Vitamin C is also important for connective tissues as well as fighting disease and absorbing iron. Fruit, potatoes and green leafy vegetables are good sources of vitamin C.

- Vitamin D is important for growth and the maintenance of bones and teeth. It helps the absorption of calcium.

Growing children need plenty of vitamins.

Minerals

The body also needs minerals in very small amounts. They are necessary for all the chemical processes that go on in the body that result in growth, energy production and development. Minerals include iron, sodium, potassium, calcium, magnesium and phosphorus. They are involved in:

- the structure of bones and teeth (calcium and fluoride);

- muscle contraction (calcium);

- nerve conduction and fluid balance in the body (sodium and potassium);

- energy processes (iron);

- enzyme formation (zinc and copper). Enzymes are compounds that speed up chemical reactions.

Iron is particularly important for exercise because it plays an important part in the production of energy. It is a component of haemoglobin, the compound in the blood that carries oxygen. A lack of iron will affect the amount of oxygen carried around the body. This can affect performance, especially in endurance-type activities.

Calcium is an important mineral for bone strength. If the body's calcium levels are low, the body starts to use the calcium from the bones and this makes them weaker and leads to **osteoporosis**. A hormone produced during menstruation (periods) helps protect the bones from this happening. However, older women who no longer have periods – and some young women who train so hard that they stop having periods – lack this hormone. This weakens their bones and may increase the chance of fractures.

Water

Water is essential for all the body's functions. It makes up about two-thirds of the body's mass: that's about 47 kilograms (47 litres) for someone who weighs about 70 kilograms.

Water is a major component of many cells and is vital for:

- transporting nutrients, waste products and hormones around and out of the body;

- temperature regulation, absorbing heat and transferring it to your skin for release to the environment. Sweating is part of this process.

Water is lost from the body through urine, faeces, expired air and sweating.

If this water is not replaced, the result is dehydration. This means that the body does not have enough water to function properly. When you feel thirsty, that's your body's way of telling you that it needs more water. By this stage the lack of water will already have started to affect your body so it is better to drink fluids regularly to avoid feeling thirsty.

It is important that you take in extra fluid before, during and after exercise. However, drinking large quantities of fluid can cause discomfort so it is better to drink a little but often.

Minerals

Minerals exist naturally in rivers, lakes, oceans, soil and rocks beneath the Earth's surface. Water that is taken from natural springs can contain many minerals. In recent years there has been a huge increase in the sale of mineral water.

Many sportspeople drink special sports drinks. These contain some carbohydrates to provide energy. They also have electrolytes. These are mineral salts (containing sodium, potassium and magnesium) that control the balance of fluids in the body.

Drinking water and other suitable fluids during exercise will help to prevent dehydration. Here Kerry McCann of Australia takes a drink during a women's marathon race at the Melbourne 2006 Commonwealth Games. Many top athletes prefer to make their own 'special' drink.

A healthy diet

It is impossible to give exact information about what you should eat to follow a healthy diet. Everyone is an individual, with their own energy requirements and food likes and dislikes.

Daily intakes

It is not possible to state the exact amount of a nutrient that anyone needs. However, the government has issued some guidelines called **recommended daily allowances** (RDA). You might also see guidelines daily amounts (GDAs) or dietary reference values (DRVs) listed for foods.

A recommended daily allowance is the amount of a nutrient most people need in order to stay healthy. Some people, such as those suffering with certain illnesses, may need different amounts. That is why the guidelines should be taken as generalizations that will vary slightly, depending on factors such as age, size and growth rate.

General guidelines

These guidelines are useful when your diet is being analysed by a nutritionist or dietician. However, they are less helpful in working out a healthy diet for yourself. It would be practically impossible to add up how much of each nutrient you eat, to check if your diet is healthy. It is easier to look at how much of your diet is made up by each of the main nutrients (carbohydrate, fat and protein) and by the food groups (shown on page 31).

Dietary analyses have been carried out to estimate the quality of the average person's diet in the UK. Guidelines or goals have also been set in terms of the percentage intake of the main nutrients.

The main health problems are:

• coronary heart disease

• cancer

• obesity.

For example, the level of fat intake (including cholesterol) in Western countries is much higher than in countries in Asia. People in these countries eat a lot more carbohydrate than westerners and heart disease is usually less common. From the table below, you can see that in general people eat too much fat and not enough carbohydrate.

Food labels

Many nutrition labels on food packets tell you what percentage of the recommended daily allowance you get from eating a portion of that food. For example, a cereal packet might tell you that eating a 30 g serving of the cereal with 125 ml of semi-skimmed milk will give you 25 per cent of the recommended daily intake of vitamin D.

	Carbohydrate (%)	Fat (%)	Protein (%)
Current	40–45	40–45	10–15
Recommended	more than 50	30	10–15

Current and recommended percentage energy intakes for the UK.

The following tips can help you make healthier food choices:

- eat less saturated fat and sugar

- base your meals on starchy foods

- eat more fish

- eat lots of fruit and vegetables

- eat less salt

- drink plenty of water

- don't skip breakfast

In 2006 the Government introduced a National Healthy School Status. This is a guide for schools to include healthy eating provision: schools were given specific rules for providing school meals. The guide came as a response to eating disorders becoming more frequent in young people.

Guidance regarding healthy eating can be found on the following websites:
www.lhps.org
www.wiredforhealth.gov.uk
www.foodinschool.org.uk
www.5aday.nhs.uk

Fruit and vegetables
You should eat at least five portions of a variety of fruit and vegetables every day.

Bread, other cereals, and potatoes
These are starchy foods, such as rice and pasta.

Milk and dairy foods
These are a good source of protein and calcium. This group includes soya alternatives for vegetarians. You should eat them in moderate amounts.

Meat, fish, and alternatives
These foods, which include beans, nuts, and pulses, contain lots of **protein**. But you should not eat too much of them.

Foods containing fat; foods containing sugar
Try not to eat too much in this group. It contains cakes, biscuits, crisps, and soft drinks.

Marathon runners need a large energy intake to fuel training and competition.

Energy requirements

The amount of food that you should eat depends on the amount of energy that you need. Your body needs energy for:

• muscle contractions

• sending nerve impulses

• digesting food

• transporting things around the body

• growth and maintenance of cells.

The amount of energy that your body uses just while you are resting is called your **basal metabolic rate**. This energy is used to keep you breathing, keep your heart beating and generally keep you alive. Each person's basal (basic) metabolic rate will vary, depending on their body's energy needs. Larger people will need more energy to keep them alive and will have a higher basal metabolic rate.

Every day you will spend a lot of energy just on normal activities such as moving around, thinking, eating and talking. Some people have very active jobs that mean they spend a lot of energy at work. Others will get very little exercise at work.

Energy will also be expended doing certain leisure activities. Many people spend their leisure time doing exercise such as cycling, walking, skateboarding, climbing and dancing. Others are involved in sports and games that require quite a lot of energy.

These activities will affect how much energy is needed by the body. Even if two people do the same activities, they might need different amounts of energy because of differences in their age and body size, as well as their gender. Men have higher basal metabolic rates than women so they need more energy than women.

Energy balance

It is important to maintain a balance between the amount of energy you take in (food) and the amount of energy you spend (output). Energy balance is achieved when:

energy intake = energy output

If you take in more energy than you spend, the extra energy is converted to fat and stored in your body. If this continues over a period of time, the amount of body fat will gradually increase and could lead to obesity and other health problems.

If you take in less energy than you need, your body has to get the extra energy from its stores. This energy can come from your body's stores of fat and carbohydrate. Your body cannot store much carbohydrate so if this continues, its store will rapidly run out. As carbohydrate is an important source of energy, this will affect your ability to exercise. Your body can store a lot of fat but if these stores are used continually, they will gradually run out.

If your body continues to get less energy than it needs, it may start to use the protein in the muscles and tissues to get energy. This happens to people who are starving, or those with eating disorders. The person's body looks very skinny as there is little fat left and the muscles are also reduced in size.

Weight control

Many people eat more fat than they need. This leads to them having excess fat levels, which can cause health problems. In order to lose this extra fat, people need either to increase the amount of energy they spend or to decrease the amount of energy they take in. The best method is to combine increased exercise with decreased energy intake, in particular decreased fat intake. This needs to be done gradually and sensibly if the change is going to be a permanent one.

In order to put on weight, people need to increase their healthy food intake or decrease the energy they spend. In this case it is probably better to eat more food than reduce exercise. Exercise has other health benefits so it is better not to reduce it, unless you are doing excessive amounts of exercise.

Weight loss

Many advertised dietary aids claim to result in rapid weight loss in short periods of time. However, people should aim to lose only 1 kg (1–2 lbs) per week. Any weight loss greater than this is probably only water.

People should only undertake a programme of sustained weight loss under the guidance of a health professional.

Judo players need to control their weight as they compete in weight categories.

Although there are many benefits to be gained from being active, there are also some risks associated with exercise. However, if you choose appropriate activities and take into consideration the safety factors, the risk of an accident or injury can be reduced.

Many light activities, such as walking, bear little risk of injury. However, several factors need to be considered before you take part in more strenuous exercise. If you think through these carefully, the risk of injury will be reduced. Some of these factors relate to general activities and some are more to do with sport.

Current health

During exercise the body has to work harder, so people with a specific health problem may need to consult a doctor before taking up an exercise programme. For example, for people with certain health problems, exercise of the wrong type or intensity could worsen their condition or put them at risk of further problems. People with asthma, diabetes, heart problems or who are obese may need to consult a doctor before doing certain physical activities.

Fitness

Whether you are exercising for health or performance reasons, it is important that you do not try to do too much exercise too soon. If you have not been very active, you should start with gentle exercise. As your fitness improves you can gradually increase the intensity or amount of exercise that you do. In this way you will be able to increase fitness without putting too much strain on your body. If you do too much too soon then you might get injured.

Even if you have been active you may need to improve your fitness before taking on a greater physical challenge. Often people decide to take up an activity to get fit, when they really need to be fit before they start that activity. In sports where there is physical contact between players, you could easily be injured if you come up against someone who is physically fitter and stronger than you.

In many activities, you need to know your limits of fitness and work within those limits. For example, if you tackle a long rock-climbing route without having the necessary level of fitness, you are more likely to fall. Although the safety rope will save you, you may still be injured during the fall.

Once you have considered these factors and have decided to do an activity, you need to think about a different set of concerns.

Jewellery

In some activities such as walking, it does not matter whether you wear jewellery or not. However, in most other activities it can be dangerous and put you or your opponent at risk of injury. In any activity where you come into contact with another person or are at risk from an injury, you should not wear jewellery. Many sports have rules that state that all jewellery must be removed.

If you are injured and are wearing jewellery, it may cause problems. If you hurt your finger and it swells, a ring could cause further problems and may have to be cut off. In contact sports a watch or other jewellery could cut or injure another player. In dance, jewellery could get caught on another dancer or on an item of clothing.

Warm-up

A warm-up is an important part of any physical activity. It helps you prepare your body physically and mentally for the activity you are about to do. A warm-up needs to start gently and be carried out in a controlled manner to be of most benefit.

Physical state

In some activities you may need to tie long hair up or cut your nails short before participating. In netball, for example, the umpires must check the length of the players' fingernails before a match. This is to prevent players being scratched or cut by each other's long nails.

Rules

It is important for physical activities involving a number of people to have clear rules and guidelines and to be well controlled so that everyone can participate safely. If everyone sticks to the rules and plays fairly, unnecessary injuries will be prevented.

The officials in sport have a responsibility to ensure that players abide by the rules and that an activity is safe. In contact sports it is important that opposing teams are matched according to age, body size or level of experience. That is why there are age groups for children's activities and weight categories for martial arts, for example.

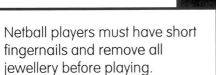

Netball players must have short fingernails and remove all jewellery before playing.

Equipment

Many physical activities, such as walking, require little special equipment. For others, it is essential to have correct equipment, to prevent injury. Equipment for an activity may range from general items of clothing to special protective suits. In every case it is essential to use the correct equipment and to make sure it is in good condition. For example, there is no point in wearing a helmet so old that it will crack on impact.

Helmets

There are many different types of helmet, for different purposes. Players of American football wear helmets to protect their heads during high-speed collisions with other players. Cyclists and rock-climbers wear helmets to protect their heads in the event of a fall, whereas canoeists wear them in case they capsize and bang their heads on rocks under the water. Helmets are compulsory for young people batting in cricket.

Footwear

Correct footwear is important even for people who do not do much exercise. Shoes or boots need to fit well and provide some cushioning. Many people get painful blisters and other problems with their feet from footwear that does not fit properly. You need to select carefully the shoe that is appropriate for your activity rather than choosing a shoe because it looks good or because it is cheap.

Footwear that has been worn a lot will not offer the same protection or cushioning as it did when it was new. Old, worn-out shoes need to be replaced.

Gum shields

These are mainly worn in sports such as hockey, rugby and boxing, where there is a risk of being hit on the mouth. It is important that the gum shield fits properly, so ideally you should consult your dentist.

Canoeists must wear a helmet in case they capsize.

Protective padding

In cricket, football, hockey and American football, players use various forms of padding to protect them from injury. Cricketers wear leg pads, gloves and arm pads as well as a helmet to protect them when batting or wicket-keeping. Footballers and hockey players wear shin pads. Hockey goalkeepers also wear leg pads, body pads and helmets to protect them. It is important that the equipment is worn properly and kept in good condition for it to be effective.

Safety equipment

People who take part in outdoor activities use extra safety equipment to protect them. Canoeists and sailors wear buoyancy aids or life-jackets in case they fall into the water. Rock-climbers and mountaineers wear harnesses with ropes attached for safety in the event of a fall.

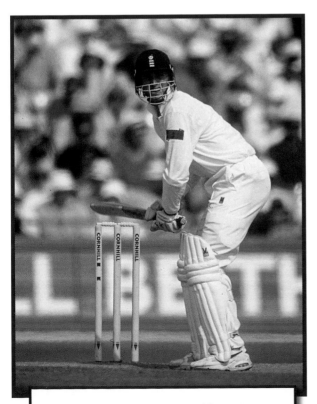

This cricketer is protected from injury by his helmet and padding.

General equipment

Equipment such as rackets, hockey sticks and cricket bats needs to be carefully maintained. Blisters and splinters can be avoided if equipment is given proper care. Goal posts in rugby and fixed posts in netball need to be covered by protective padding in case a player collides with them.

Handling equipment

When heavy equipment has to be moved, great care must be taken to avoid injuries. There are usually set procedures for handling large items such as trampolines, gymnastic equipment and canoes so that the risk of injury is reduced. It is important to learn these procedures before attempting to handle the equipment.

Environment

The weather is a major factor that often affects physical activities. It can also affect safety, and so must always be taken into consideration. Strong winds, rain, snow or cold weather are potentially dangerous. Being caught in bad weather in the mountains or at sea can lead to people getting lost, especially if visibility is poor. It is important to check weather reports before setting out and to be aware of any changes occurring during the expedition.

Most sports that are played outdoors can be affected by the weather. Matches may have to be called off due to poor visibility or unsafe conditions. Wet surfaces can be hazardous because they become slippery. Hard, dry ground can be a problem if players cannot get a grip or if they fall on the ground. The referee or umpire usually makes the decision whether a match can start or if it should continue. Part of their job is to ensure the playing conditions are safe for everyone.

Causes of injury

Injuries can be caused in many ways and occur for a variety of reasons. The two main categories of injuries are:

- **traumatic injuries**
- **over-use injuries.**

Traumatic injuries

These injuries occur suddenly and you can usually feel that something significant has gone wrong. There may be immediate signs of injury such as swelling, pain and bruising. The injuries may be caused by external factors, such as a collision with another person, or by internal factors, such as a pulled muscle. Internal factors are not related to another person and may not have an obvious cause.

External causes

Depending on the nature of the activity there could be a variety of external causes of injury:

- Impact injuries occur as a result of a collision with another person or a piece of equipment. These are more likely to occur in sports than in outdoor activities, dance or swimming. All contact sports, such as rugby and football, involve impacts between players. This means that players have a greater chance of being injured in this way. In a sport such as boxing

the main aim is to hurt your opponent, so the risk of an injury is very high. In these activities it is essential that players are physically fit enough for the competition. The contest should be between similar groups. For example a schoolboy rugby team should not be expected to play against a good adult club side, because the differences in physical size would make injuries to the schoolboys very likely.

- Collisions with equipment may also result in injuries. This may happen when a player runs into a goal post, is hit by a hockey stick or injured by a cricket ball. Gymnasts may collide with equipment if they mistime

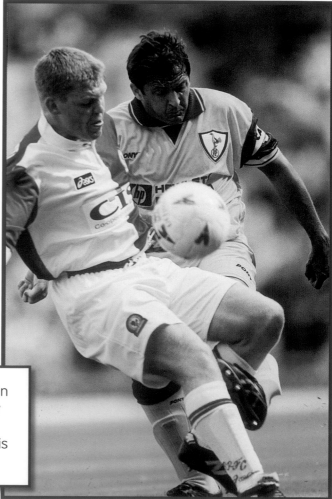

Impact injuries are common in contact sports, such as rugby and football. Former football player Gary Mabbutt broke his leg in this collision.

Collisions with equipment can cause injuries. Rugby posts are padded to protect players who might be moving fast or pushed into them. In 2006 England's Mark Cueto made this spectacular dive between the posts to score a try against Italy.

the execution of a move. Bruising and cuts are the most likely result of an impact, but more serious injuries such as dislocations, fractures and concussion may occur.

- Playing surfaces may cause injuries when a player falls on or slides across the surface. This can result in cuts and grazes from tarmac surfaces or friction burns from an artificial surface. When playing on uneven surfaces such as a rough patch of grass, a player may twist an ankle by landing awkwardly.

On some surfaces, ankle injuries occur when someone tries to stop suddenly and there is no slip in the surface. This means that the player's foot does not slide, even slightly. Sometimes just a little amount of slide helps the player not to go over on their ankle.

- Equipment – minor injuries may occur as a result of using a piece of equipment even though it is not faulty. Blisters are common, particularly when you are using new shoes or a new racket, for example. Even if the equipment is not new, if it is used for a prolonged length of time an injury might occur.

- Accidents – the main aim of any safety precautions is to reduce the likelihood of accidents. However, no matter how many precautions are taken, accidents will still happen. Some activities carry higher risks of injury than others. In dancing or ice skating, there is always the risk of slipping or of one performer dropping the other. The person doing the lift needs to be strong enough to hold the other person. Such accidents may be rare but preparation is still an important part of minimizing the risk.

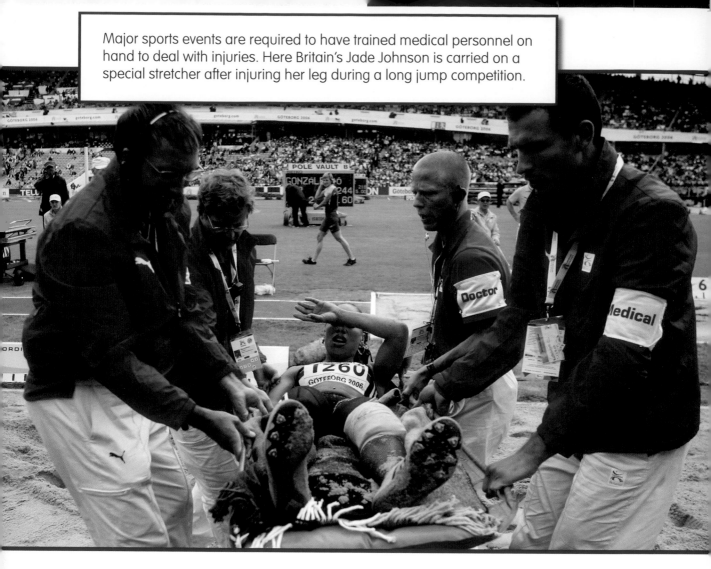

Major sports events are required to have trained medical personnel on hand to deal with injuries. Here Britain's Jade Johnson is carried on a special stretcher after injuring her leg during a long jump competition.

Some activities are more risky than others. Outdoor activities such as rock-climbing, canoeing and skiing have an element of risk involved, which is why they appeal to many people. They like the challenge of the activity and get a great deal of satisfaction from overcoming the elements. However, participants have to be aware of the risks and make a decision as to whether they wish to take the chance of having an accident. The more risks they take, the more serious the injury is likely to be if something goes wrong.

Internal causes

An injury may occur without prior warning during any physical activity, and it may be difficult to know what caused it. The most common type of injury is a sprain or strain. The injury may be due to over-stretching or twisting in an awkward way. A lot of back injuries occur when people try to lift an object using an incorrect technique.

Fatigue, illness, stiffness and pain are all warning signs that must be heeded. The chance of internal injuries occurring is greater when you are feeling like this.

Over-use injuries

These injuries build up gradually over time, and that may make them harder to diagnose. They are often a result of doing a certain activity or action over and over again. Some of these injuries could be avoided by structuring training programmes, competition schedules or activity sessions appropriately and taking adequate rest between sessions. There are several very common over-use injuries:

• Tennis elbow is a common injury among tennis players but can occur as a result of other sports or even from everyday activities. It is a strain of a tendon on the outer side of the elbow and is usually due to over-working or straining the muscles of the forearm.

• Golfer's elbow is a similar type of injury to tennis elbow but affects the tendon on the inside of the elbow.

• Shin splints is a general term to describe pain in the front and side of the lower leg. It is often associated with running or walking long distances. Wearing correct footwear may help avoid this injury.

• Stress fractures occur as a result of an increase in the work load on a certain bone. Runners may suffer stress fractures in the leg if they do too much running or wear incorrect footwear. Stress fractures may also be caused by muscle or tendon injuries that pull at the bone and cause a fracture to occur.

It is important that these types of injuries are treated early, to prevent more serious damage. Continuing to do an activity when you know you have an injury will make the situation worse and may put you out of action for longer than is necessary.

Tennis elbow is a common injury among tennis players. It is caused by the large forces involved in hitting a tennis ball and repeating the movement over a long period of time.

You should know something about some of the injuries you may come across when involved in physical activity. Some minor injuries can be dealt with fairly easily. Others are more serious and should only be dealt with by a qualified first-aider, physiotherapist or doctor. Even if the initial injury does not need immediate medical attention, it is always a good idea to get the injury checked by a doctor afterwards, particularly if the pain or swelling persists.

Medical help should be sent for immediately if any of these things happen:

- an injured person is unconscious

- a fracture is suspected

- a back or neck injury is suspected. **In this case the person should not be moved**.

If in doubt as to what to do, it is better to do nothing and send for help immediately, rather than do the wrong thing. Some common injuries that you might come across in relation to physical activity are explained below.

Bruising

Bruises are caused by internal bleeding from blood vessels that have been damaged, often due to impact. Bruising may occur hours or days after the injury but if it occurs soon after the injury then there may be deeper injury.

Applying ice to the injury will reduce the flow of blood to the area and reduce the amount of internal bleeding and bruising.

Cuts

With any cut there is a risk of infection from dirt or germs entering the wound. In the case of a minor cut, the area around it should be cleaned and a sterile (clean) dressing applied until bleeding stops. The cut should then be covered with a plaster. If bleeding is severe, the body part should be raised and supported to reduce the flow of blood to the area. A clean dressing should be applied, with gentle pressure, to try to stem the flow of blood.

If the wound is large, stitches may be required so the casualty should be taken quickly to a nearby hospital.

Sprain

When damage occurs to a ligament, the injury is called a sprain. Ligaments join bone to bone in a joint and provide the joint with strength and stability. When a joint is forced beyond its normal range of movement, the ligaments are over-stretched and a sprain occurs. If the ligament is torn, the casualty may have heard a snapping sound. This can make it difficult to know whether it is a torn ligament or a fracture. If in doubt deal with it as if it is a fracture.

Strain

When a muscle is partially torn, the injury is called a strain. This can occur as a result of over-stretching a muscle. The injury is usually painful when touched and flexibility might be reduced. You should never try to force the muscle to stretch as this could cause further injury.

Fracture

A fracture is a crack or break in a bone. Fractures can be caused by a direct force, such as a heavy blow, or by an indirect force. With an indirect force, the force may travel from the point of impact through the body and fracture a bone somewhere else. A sudden twist or wrench is also an indirect force that may fracture a bone.

There are different types of fracture and some are more serious than others:

- Open fracture – the broken bone has pierced the skin and it may be sticking out.

- Closed fracture – there is no damage to the skin but there might be bruising and swelling.

The casualty may have heard a snapping sound or felt a sharp pain. They will have difficulty moving the limb and it will be painful to do. The limb may be distorted, bruised, swollen or all three. If you suspect a fracture, you should not try to move that part of the body. It may need to be immobilized by use of a splint. The injury will need to be treated by a doctor so you should send for an ambulance.

Blood rules

Many sports have brought in rules about what to do if a player is bleeding. Usually the player must leave the game until the wound has been cleaned and covered. This is particularly important in sports where people will come into contact with each other. This rule has been introduced mainly because of the concern over HIV and AIDS, but also to prevent the spread of other infections.

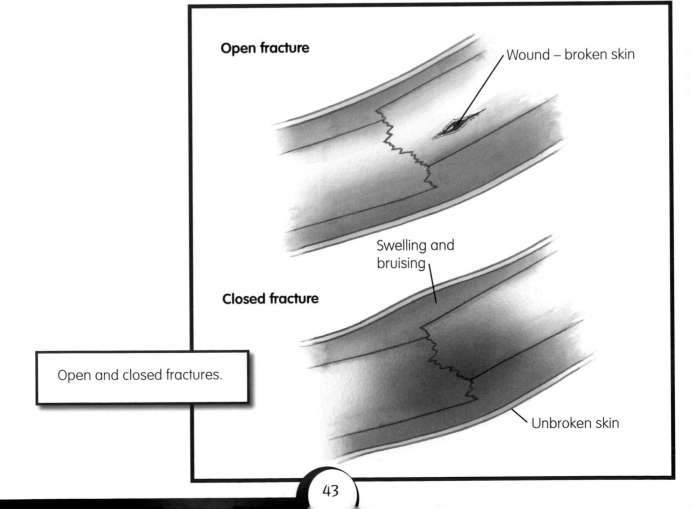

Open fracture

Wound – broken skin

Swelling and bruising

Closed fracture

Unbroken skin

Open and closed fractures.

Dislocation

In a dislocation, a bone comes out of its normal position. This may be due to a strong force or muscle contraction wrenching the bone out of position. Dislocations occur most commonly in the shoulder, thumb, finger and jaw. As with fractures, the affected area should not be moved and the casualty should be taken to hospital.

Head injuries

The brain is a very sensitive organ. Any damage to the head could affect the brain and is therefore, potentially dangerous. A person with a head injury should not continue the activity, but should be checked by a doctor. If the casualty loses consciousness, this may be due to damage to the skull, the brain or blood vessels inside the brain. You should place the casualty in the recovery position and send for an ambulance.

Concussion

Concussion is a brief loss of consciousness, usually caused by a blow to the head. When conscious the casualty may feel dizzy, have a headache and even suffer loss of memory. If they regain consciousness quickly, they should not continue the activity, but you should watch them carefully and make sure they are examined by a doctor. If the casualty remains unconscious you should place them in the recovery position and send for an emergency ambulance.

RICE

The RICE procedure is a simple method of treating bruises, sprains and strains. The aim is to reduce swelling and pain. This may be the only treatment that is required for minor injuries but further medical attention may be needed:

Rest – the injured part should be rested so the activity should not be continued.

Ice – apply ice to the affected area. This will help reduce swelling, bruising and pain.

Compression – apply gentle, even pressure to the area. Cover the area with a thick layer of sterile (clean) cotton wool and keep it in place with a bandage. Be careful not to make it too tight.

Elevation – raise and support the injured part. This reduces the blood flow to the area and will reduce bruising.

Skin infections and disorders

Skin infections can be quite common among people who take part in physical activity:

- A verruca, or plantar wart, is a wart that occurs on feet. It is contagious, which means it can spread from one person to another very easily, so great care must be taken to avoid this. There are creams available to treat a verruca but you may need to consult your doctor.

- Athlete's foot does not just happen in athletes but is common among them. It is a type of fungus that grows on the feet and causes itching and broken skin. Like verrucas it is highly contagious.

If you have athlete's foot or a verruca you should not walk around in bare feet or share your towel or shoes with anyone else, in case you pass the infection to them. Creams and powders can be used to help treat the area.

Any open wound or burst blister needs to be kept clean so that infection does not set in and make the wound worse.

A blister is caused by something rubbing against the skin or by a burn. You should never burst a blister as this could lead to infection. Some blisters will burst naturally. These should be covered to reduce the chance of infection. Attention to hygiene can help avoid some of these problems.

Environmental injuries

Some injuries are caused by weather conditions such as temperature, cold winds or snow. These can happen to anyone who is exercising outdoors. However, those involved in mountaineering, climbing, sailing and canoeing are more likely to encounter these problems.

Hypothermia

This condition sets in when the body temperature falls below 35°C (normal body temperature is about 37°C). This may be caused by being outdoors in cold weather for a long time but may also affect people in the home, particularly the elderly or very young.

Hyperthermia

This condition occurs when the body temperature gets too high. This can happen when exercising in the heat. If the body is unable to get rid of the extra heat being produced, the body temperature will increase. This can result in heat exhaustion or heat stroke. Heat exhaustion can build up gradually and results in feeling dizzy, with headaches, sweating and cramps. The casualty needs to be cooled down and rested. Heat stroke is more sudden and the body starts to overheat dangerously. Body temperature exceeds 40°C and medical attention is needed.

The recovery position.

Glossary

aerobic endurance ability to keep exercising while using oxygen to supply energy

agility ability to perform rapidly a movement of the body, or part of it

amino acids simple units that make up proteins. They are used for the manufacture of the structure of many tissues, haemoglobin, hormones and enzymes.

atherosclerosis medical name for the build-up of fat in an artery

balance ability to keep control of the body

basal metabolic rate amount of energy that is used by your body while you are resting just to keep you alive

body composition percentage of fat or lean body mass (anything that is not fat) that make up the body

carbohydrates nutrients that supply your body with energy

cardiovascular to do with the the heart and blood vessels that carry blood around the body

cholesterol substance found in certain types of fat. It is essential for a healthy body, but too much may cause atherosclerosis.

complex carbohydrates (starches) carbohydrates made up of many sugar units, for example bread, rice, pasta and vegetables

co-ordination ability to put together a series of movements in an organized fashion such as in a dance

coronary heart disease when an artery supplying the heart becomes partially or completely blocked due to atherosclerosis

drug abuse using drugs when there is no health reason for doing so or taking more of a drug than is needed; drug abuse can be very harmful to health

essential amino acids amino acids that cannot be made by the body so must be obtained from the diet

fat important nutrient stored in the body, providing insulation, protection and energy

fatigue symptom that occurs when the body is not able to supply the energy that is needed for exercise

fibre non-digestible carbohydrate that forms the skeleton of plant cells. It is not absorbed by the body but it is essential for the digestive system work to properly.

flexibility range of movement at a joint or series of joints

health-related fitness fitness achieved when people wish to be fit in order to live a full and healthy life

hormone replacement therapy (HRT) method of replacing hormones that are no longer made in the body. HRT is used to prevent osteoporosis.

hypertension medical term for high blood pressure

lean body mass portion of body mass left when body fat has been subtracted from total body mass; made up of bones, muscles, blood and organs

masking agent chemical that can mask, or hide, the presence of steroids or other drugs in the body

maximum strength maximum force produced in one effort

menopause phase during which a woman no longer menstruates (has periods) regularly

minerals necessary for all the chemical processes that result in growth, energy production and development. They include iron, sodium, potassium and calcium.

muscle tone firmness of muscles developed when some muscle fibres are contracted and others are relaxed, in response to a stretch in the muscle

muscular endurance ability to perform repeated muscle contractions without tiring

non-essential amino acids amino acids that can be made by the body

obesity medical term for the condition when someone is carrying excess amounts of body fat

osteoporosis disease of the bones that causes them to break easily, often referred to as brittle bone disease

over-use injuries injuries that build up gradually over time, which may make them harder to diagnose

passive smoking inhaling other people's smoke

performance-enhancing drugs drugs that are taken to try to improve performance

performance-related fitness fitness achieved when people wish to be able to do an activity well

posture way in which the body is held

power combination of strength and speed – the ability to exert high levels of force over a short period of time

proteins nutrients needed for growth and repair of tissues. Proteins are also used to make enzymes and hormones.

pulses foods such as peas, beans and lentils, which are high in protein.

recommended daily allowance/amount how much of a nutrient most people need in order to stay healthy

saturated fat type of fat mainly found in animal products such as meat, poultry and dairy products. Saturated fats are generally considered to be unhealthy.

self esteem how you feel about yourself

side effects effects of a drug other than the main effect for which they are being taken, usually undesirable

simple carbohydrates (sugars) carbohydrates consisting of few sugar units, for example jam, marmalade, honey, sugar, sweets and biscuits

smog formed when fog mixes with the chemical emissions from cars and factories

speed ability to move the body or its parts quickly

trans fat type of fat sometimes made in food manufacturing processes. These fats are considered unhealthy.

traumatic injuries injuries that occur suddenly; you may feel something pull or break

unsaturated fat type of fat usually considered to be a healthy choice. Monounsaturated fats are found in peanuts and olive oil, for example. Polyunsaturated fats are found in sunflower oil and oily fish such as sardines.

vitamins chemical compounds needed in small amounts; they cannot be made by your body

water chemical that the body needs in order to survive. Water is an essential nutrient.

Find out more

Books

Body Talk: Move Your Body, Steve Parker (Raintree 2006)

Health Issues: Sports Injuries, Sarah Lennard-Brown (Wayland, 2006)

It's Your Health: Exercise, Adam Hibbert (Franklin Watts, 2004)

Making Healthy Food Choices: Food for Sports, Neil Morris (Heinemann Library, 2006)

Making Healthy Food Choices: Do You Know What's In Your Food?, Neil Morris (Heinemann Library, 2006)

Websites

BBC health and fitness http://news.bbc.co.uk/sport1/hi/health_and_fitness/default.stm

BBC health www.bbc.co.uk/health/healthy_living/fitness/injuries_index.shtml

British Heart Foundation www.bhf.org.uk

DrugScope, the UK's leading independent centre of expertise on drugs: www.drugscope.org.uk

Food Standards Agency www.food.gov.uk

Healthy eating advice www.eatwell.gov.uk

World Anti-Doping Agency www.wada-ama.org

Index